EVERYDAY SCI

about the weather

Barbara Taylor

photography by

Peter Millard

HODDER Wayland

an imprint of Hodder Children's Books

First published in 1997
by Macdonald Young Books

First published in
Paperback in 2001
by Hodder Wayland,
an inprint of
Hodder Children`s Books

Commissioning editor: Debbie Fox

Project editor: Caroline Wilson

Design: The Design Works, Reading

Illustrators: David Pattison, Geoff Pike

The publisher and author would like to thank Carol Olivier of Kenmont Primary School, and the following children for taking part in the photography: Sharena Ali, Danny Botross, Jason Botross, Katie Condon, Melissa Doohan, Corey Graham-Simmonds, Christopher Hayes, Sirrina Simpson-St-Aimee, Leon Swaby, Samantha Wallace, Nicole Whyte and Saffan Woods.

Thanks also to Elaine Tanner, Wendy Bray and Angela Bickerton and their classes at St James' Primary School.

Printed and bound in Portugal by: Grafiasa, Porto

A CIP catalogue record for this book is available from the British Library.

ISBN 0 7502 3516 0

Contents

Weather safety

- Never stare at the Sun or any bright light. You could damage your eyes.
- If you are caught outdoors in a thunderstorm, keep away from trees on their own or metal objects. Lightning takes the quickest path to the ground, and often runs down high objects standing alone. The safest places are inside cars or low buildings, as the electricity runs around the outside of them.
- Take care when walking on icy ground, and never walk on frozen ponds or lakes. If the ice is thin, you could easily fall into the freezing water.
- It's a good idea to wear light-coloured clothes and reflective strips in the fog so motorists can see you easily.

Where do rainbows come from?

You see a rainbow when sunlight shines through raindrops. Sunlight is made up of lots of colours – red, orange, yellow, green, blue, indigo and violet. As sunlight passes through a raindrop, it bends, or is refracted, and splits up into these colours. Red light bends least and violet bends most, so red is on the outside of a rainbow and violet is on the inside. The colours are reflected off the back of the raindrops and into your eyes.

What makes the sky go red?

In the early morning or evening, when the Sun is low, its rays have to travel a long way before they reach you. Bits of dust and gas in the sky scatter the different colours in sunlight in all directions. Colours at the blue end of the rainbow are scattered more than red colours. More red light gets through to your eyes, making the sky look red, orange or pink.

Did you know that people have sometimes seen as many as eight rainbows in the sky at once?

Why does the Sun go down at night?

The Sun doesn't really move. It is the Earth that spins around all the time – once every 24 hours. When your part of the Earth turns away from the Sun, it looks as if the Sun is going down. It gets dark, and you have night-time.

Why is sunshine hot?

The Sun gives out heat because it is a ball of very hot gases. The temperature in the middle of the Sun is more than 15 million degrees centigrade. You can't actually see this heat, but it makes the Sun so hot that it glows, and gives off light, which you can see. The Sun's heat makes the air move and causes the weather.

Did you know that the Ancient Greeks believed that the Sun god Hellos drove his chariot across the sky during the day? He rested his horses at night.

Why is it cold at the Poles?

To reach the North and South Poles, the Sun's rays have to travel further than they do to reach the equator. So on the way, they lose some heat. The rays also hit the Poles at a slanting angle. So they have to heat a wider area, and lose even more heat. When the rays reach the Poles, the snow and ice reflect away most of their remaining heat.

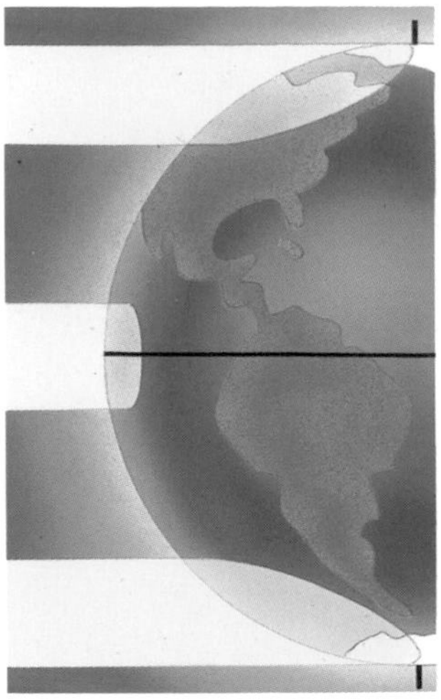

The Sun's rays hit the Earth at different angles because the Earth is curved. They heat the equator more than the Poles.

Why is is hot in a rainforest?

Rainforests grow around the middle, or 'waist', of the Earth, which is called the equator. Here the Sun's rays come straight down. At the equator, a lot of the Sun's heat hits a small area of the Earth, making rainforests hot all year round. In the daytime, it is usually about 30°C. Rainforests get around two-and-a-half times more heat each day than the Poles.

Did you know that the Sun never goes down for about six months of the year at the North and South Poles?

Why are shadows longer in winter?

In winter, the Sun is low in the sky and its rays hit the ground at a shallow angle. Objects block out a lot of the light, which makes their shadows long. In summer, when the Sun is high in the sky, objects block out less light, making their shadows shorter. The position of the Sun in the sky changes with the seasons because the Earth leans at a slight angle. In warmer seasons, the Earth is leaning towards the Sun; in colder seasons, it is leaning away from it.

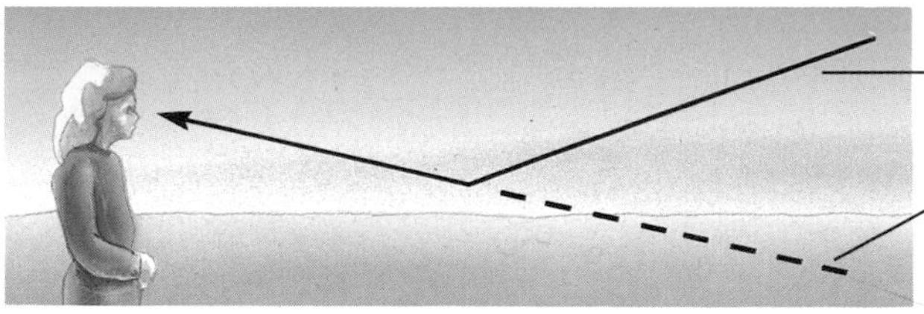

Did you know that the Moon's shadow sometimes turns day into night? When the Moon passes between the Sun and the Earth, it blocks out the sunlight and casts a huge shadow on the Earth's surface. This is called an eclipse.

Why does the road look wet and wobbly on a very hot day?

On hot days, the air near the ground is much hotter than air higher up. As sunlight passes from cooler air to warmer air, it travels faster. This makes it bend, or be refracted, upwards, so objects seem to be in a different position from where they really are. The road looks wet and wobbly because you see a picture of the sky on the ground. This trick of the light is called a mirage.

How can I tell how hot it is?

The air heats up when the Sun warms the Earth's surface and the Earth gives off heat, which warms the air above it. When the Sun shines less, the air cools down. You can use an instrument called a thermometer to measure how hot or how cold the air is. This measurement is called the temperature. Thermometers contain some mercury or alcohol, which moves up a narrow transparent tube when it gets hot and falls back again when it gets cold.

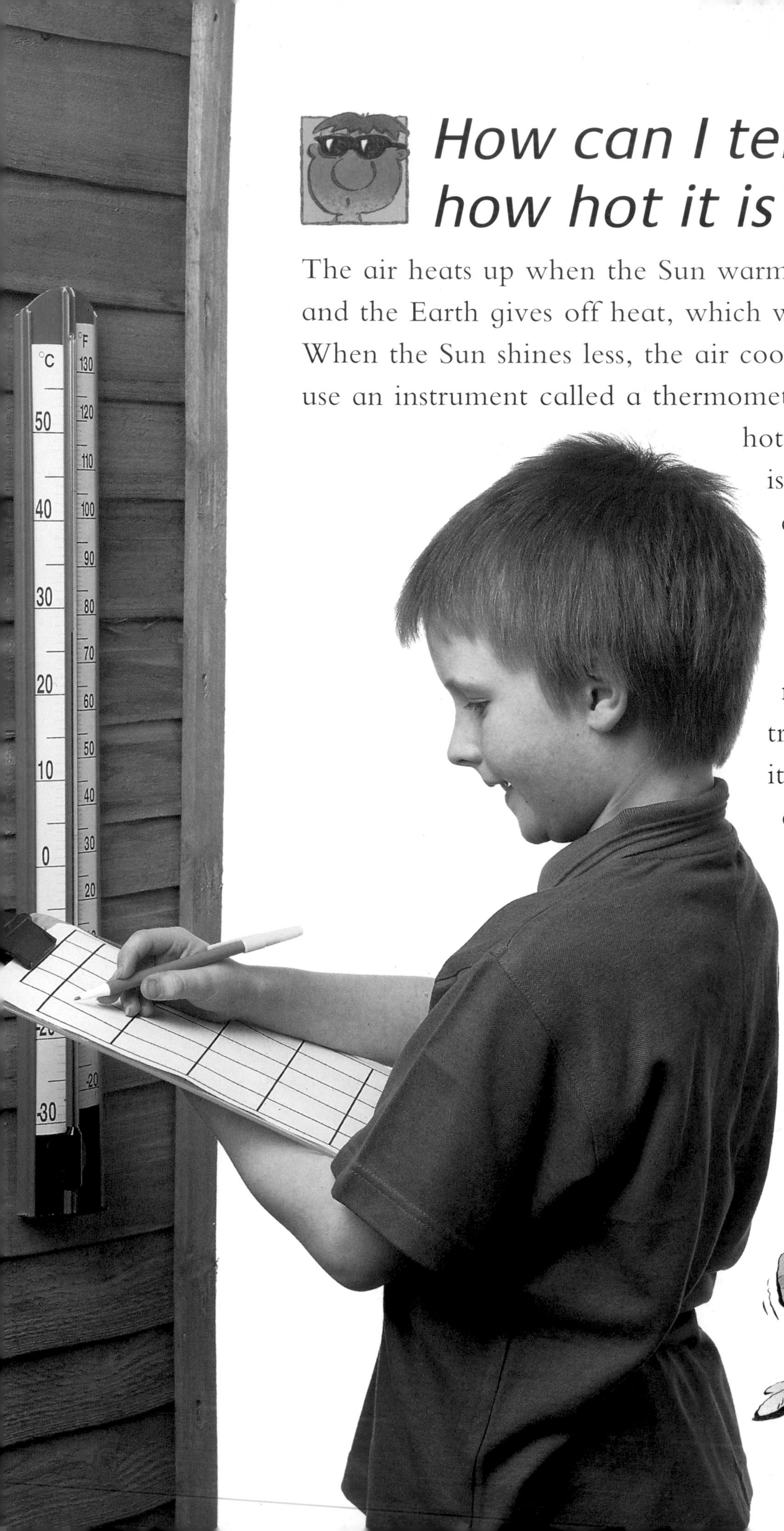

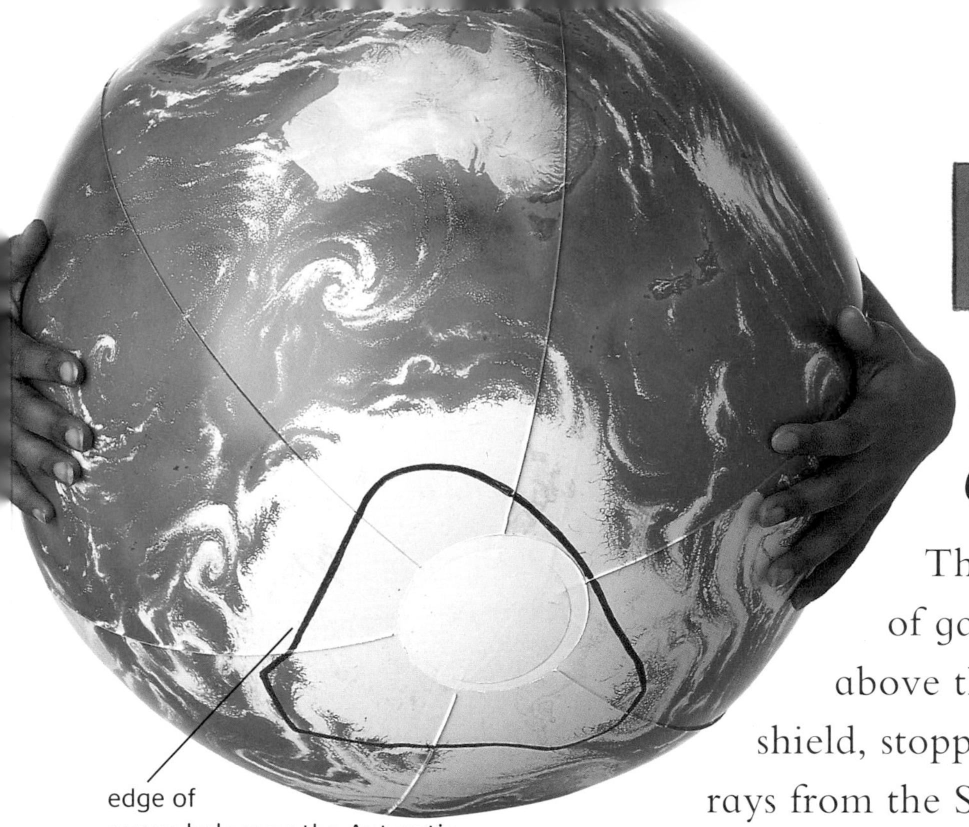

edge of
ozone hole over the Antarctic

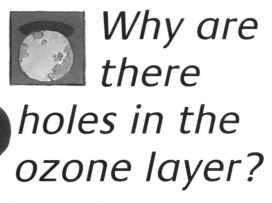

Why are there holes in the ozone layer?

The ozone layer is a layer of gas about 15–30 kilometres above the Earth. It works as a shield, stopping most of the ultra-violet rays from the Sun getting through to the Earth. Too many ultra-violet rays can cause skin cancer and eye problems in people and are also harmful to plants and animals. Scientists have shown that gases called CFCs released by factories have caused holes in the ozone layer. The holes are biggest over the Antarctic and Arctic, but there are smaller holes all over the world too.

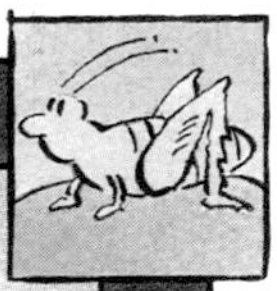

True or false?

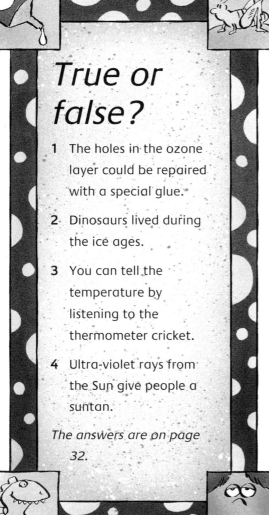

1 The holes in the ozone layer could be repaired with a special glue.

2 Dinosaurs lived during the ice ages.

3 You can tell the temperature by listening to the thermometer cricket.

4 Ultra-violet rays from the Sun give people a suntan.

The answers are on page 32.

Is the world getting warmer?

Some people believe that certain gases from car fumes and power stations are trapping the heat given off by the Earth. This is making the world warm up and is called global warming. A rise of only a few degrees in the world's temperature would melt the ice near the Poles, causing sea levels to rise. Two-thirds of the people in the world live on or near the coast, and places like London, New York and Sydney could end up underwater.

What are jet streams?

These are super-fast winds that blow about ten kilometres above the Earth. They can blow as fast as 320 kilometres per hour. Jet streams blowing from the West over the Atlantic can make planes fly faster from New York to London than in the opposite direction.

Why does the wind blow?

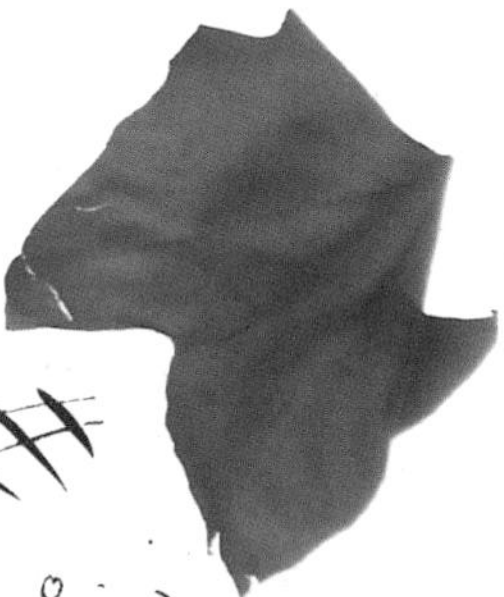

Did you know that the winds on Mount Everest can reach up to 320 kph?

The wind blows when the air around you moves from place to place. This happens when the air warms up or cools down. Air is warmed by the Sun, becomes lighter, and rises up into the sky. Cool air is sucked in to fill the space. Winds move from places with cold, sinking air to fill the spaces left by warm, rising air. The wind blows faster higher up in the sky, such as on mountain-tops.

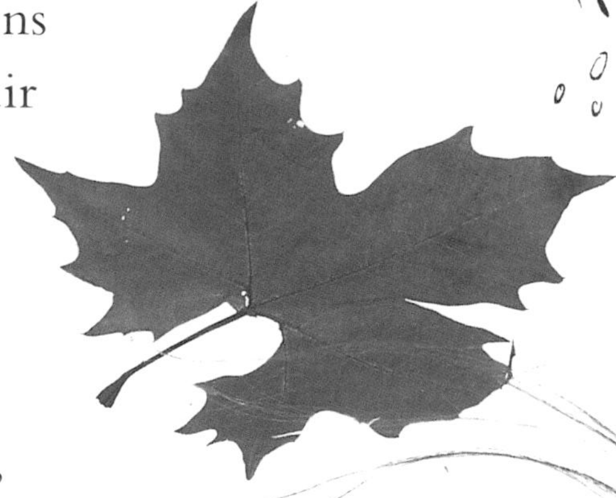

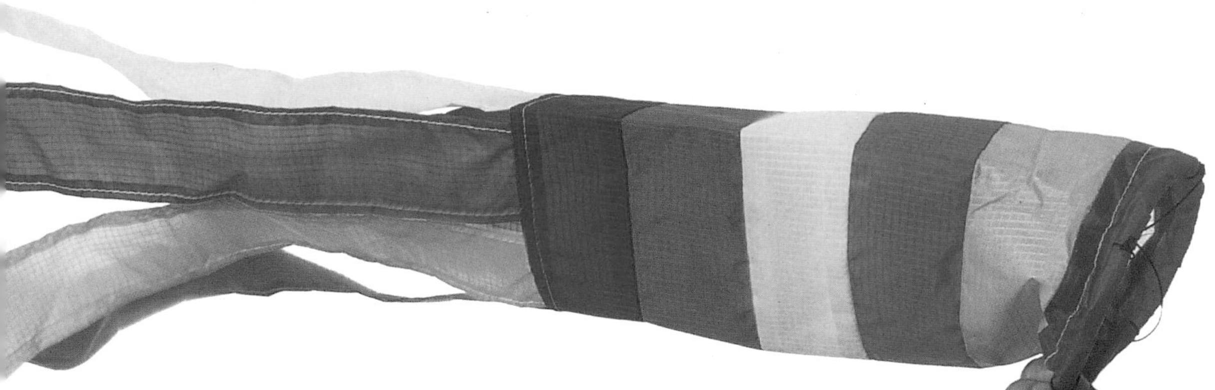

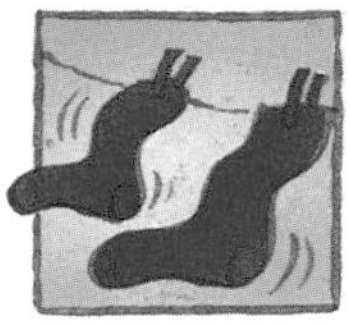

What does my windsock do?

A windsock helps to show which way the wind is blowing and how strong it is. The wind blows into the open end of the sock so the tail of the sock points the way the wind is blowing. If the sock flaps loosely, the wind is light. If the sock is stretched out in a straight line, it shows the wind is blowing strongly. Windsocks that can swivel on a tall pole are used at airports, seaports and along mountain roads.

Did you know that one modern windmill can make enough electricity for about 600 homes?

What are windfarms?

There are no animals or crops on a windfarm – only windmills! These special windmills catch the power of the wind and use it to make electricity. They do not pollute the air like power stations, which burn coal or oil. But they are quite noisy and some people think they make the countryside look ugly.

Why did tall ships have so many sails?

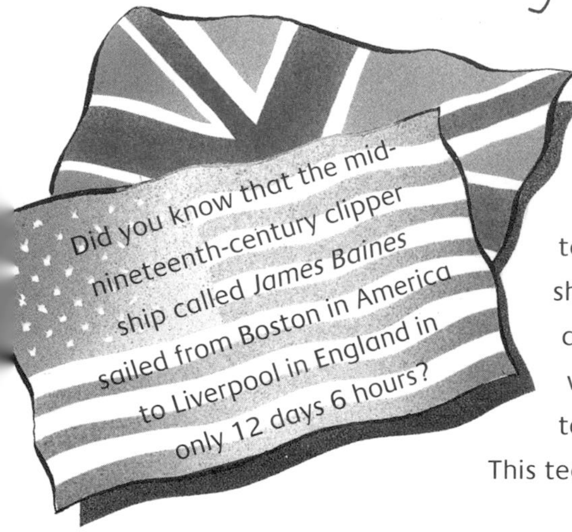

Did you know that the mid-nineteenth-century clipper ship called *James Baines* sailed from Boston in America to Liverpool in England in only 12 days 6 hours?

The more sails a ship has, the more wind it can catch and the faster it goes. In the 1850s, the fastest tall sailing ships were called clipper ships. They had three tall masts, as well as a long, sleek shape to cut through the water easily. Clipper ships raced against each other to bring the first tea of the year from China to the West. This tea could be sold for a high price.

Where is the wind coming from?

A weathervane swings round in the wind so that the tail of the arrow points in the direction the wind is coming from. Winds are usually named after the direction they come from – a north wind blows from the North. If you record the wind direction over a period of time, you can see how the weather changes with the direction of the wind. A wind blowing from the North usually brings cold weather, while winds blowing from the South are mostly warm.

What is the Beaufort scale?

The Beaufort scale divides the strength of the wind into 13 numbers, from calm at zero to hurricane force at 12. For each number, it gives the speed of the wind and the effect it has on things around us. The name comes from the person who first invented the scale nearly 200 years ago, Admiral Beaufort.

0	1	2	3	4	5	6
0 kph	3 kph	9 kph	15 kph	25 kph	35 kph	45 kph
Calm	Light air	Light breeze	Gentle breeze	Moderate wind	Fresh wind	Strong wind

7	8	9	10	11	12
56 kph	68 kph	81 kph	94 kph	110 kph	118 kph
Near gale	Gale	Severe gale	Storm	Severe storm	Hurricane

How can I measure the speed of the wind?

You can do this with something called an anemometer. The wind catches the little cups and blows them around. The faster the wind blows, the faster the cups go round. A counter records the number of times they whizz around in a certain period of time. This figure is then changed into knots or kph. A knot is 1.8 kph.

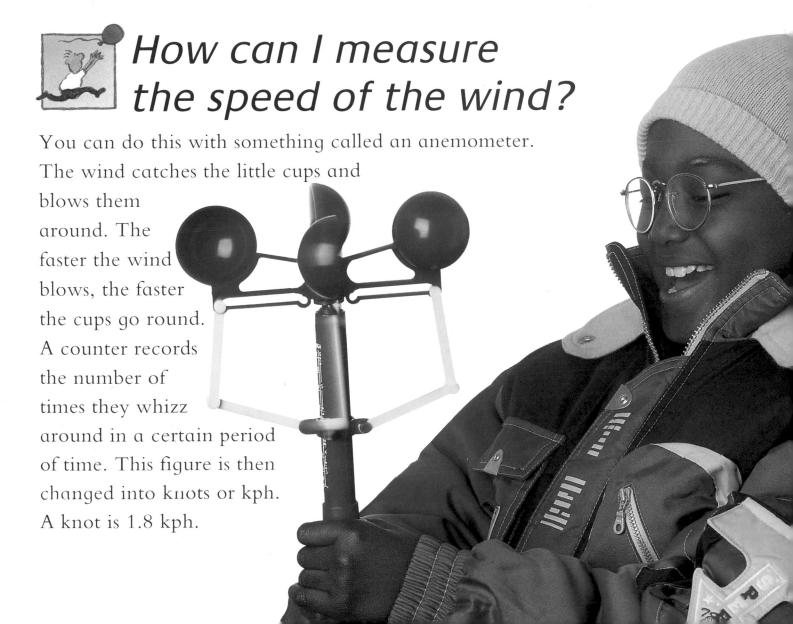

Why does it rain?

Each raindrop is made up of hundreds of thousands of tiny droplets of water. On their own, these droplets are so light that they float in the air as clouds. But sometimes, droplets fall down through the cloud, bumping into other droplets and joining up with them. These larger drops are too heavy to hang in the sky and fall out of the bottom of the clouds as rain. Rain can also be melting snow, which turns into raindrops on its way down to the ground.

True or false?

1 Frogs, spiders and fish sometimes fall from the sky when it rains.

2 No rain fell in the Atacama desert in South America for over 40 years.

3 Rain always comes from clouds.

The answers are on page 32.

How can I measure the rain?

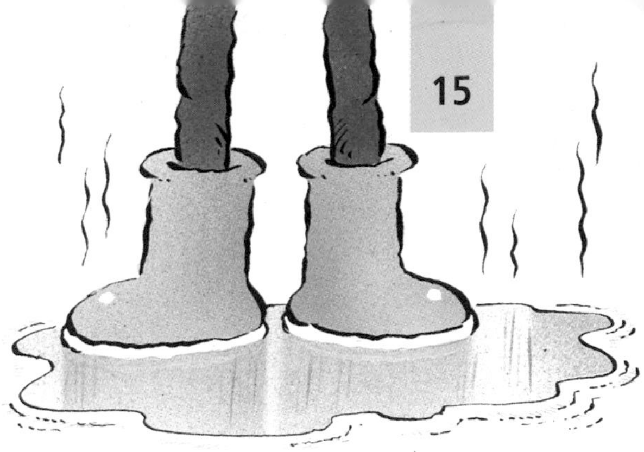

You can measure rainfall by recording how much water collects in a container called a rain gauge. Sink the container a little way into the ground, but make sure the rim is high enough to avoid water splashing up off the ground. Take records at regular intervals to build up a picture of the rainfall pattern in your area. Each time, tip the rain out of the container and measure how much you have.

Why do puddles disappear?

When the Sun heats puddles, some of the water turns into a gas called water vapour. The change from a liquid to a gas is called evaporation. Water vapour is lighter than liquid water, so it rises up into the sky and the puddle dries up and disappears.

To make a rain gauge, cut off the top of a plastic drinks bottle. Turn this upside down and balance it in the bottom part of the bottle to make a funnel.

Did you know that people have been showered with coloured rain? Occasionally, sand or dust trapped in raindrops gives rain some extra colour.

Did you know that the white trails left behind high-flying aircraft form in the same way as clouds? Hot air from the aircraft cools down and freezes to form thin cloud trails, called contrails.

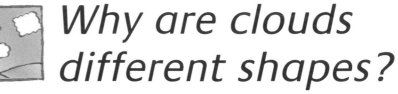

Why are clouds different shapes?

There are about ten main shapes of cloud, from wispy cirrus clouds or fluffy cumulus clouds to layers of flat stratus clouds and billowing, cauliflower-like cumulonimbus clouds. The shape of a cloud depends on how it was formed and how high in the sky it is. Cloud shape is also affected by the temperature of the air and how much moisture it contains.

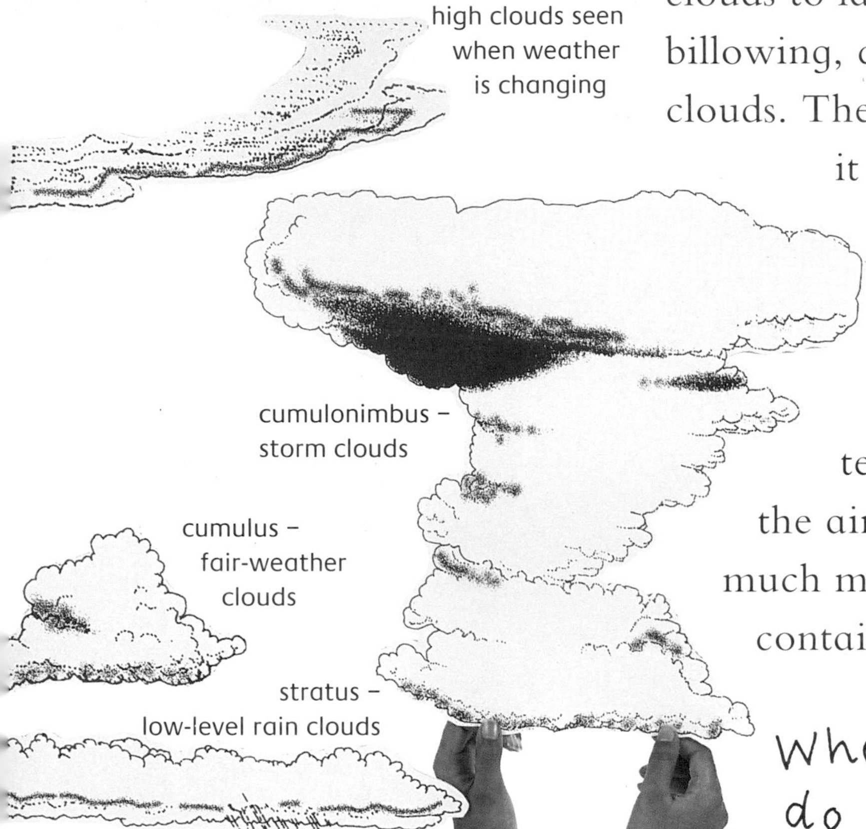

Did you know that the building used to store the space shuttles is so big it has clouds on the ceiling?

Where do clouds come from?

Clouds often form when a warm patch of the Earth's surface heats the air above it. This makes a large bubble of warm air, which rises up like a hot-air balloon. As it rises, it cools down and the water vapour in the air turns into drops of liquid water. The drops are so small and light they float in the air as clouds. Clouds also form when air rises over a mountain and cools down.

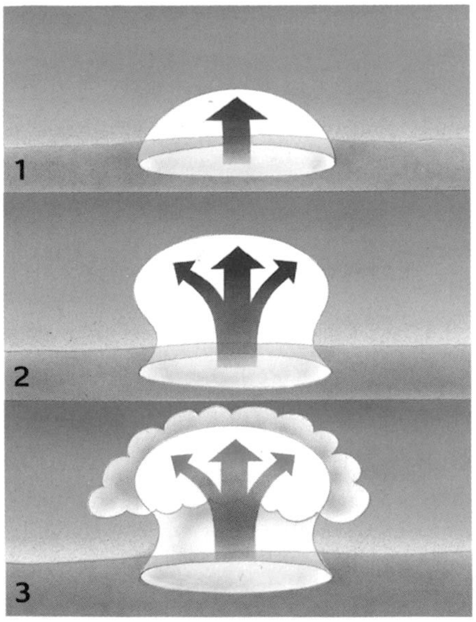

1 air heated by Earth's surface

2 bubble of warm air rises

3 air cools to form clouds

Why can't I see far in the fog?

Fog is really clouds near the ground. It forms when the surface of the ground is cooler than the air, and the cold ground cools a deep layer of air above it. The water vapour in this air condenses into very tiny drops of liquid water, which make everything look hazy and block your view. Foggy weather can be dangerous, so wearing bands that reflect light make it easier for people to see you in fog.

What is smog?

Smog is a kind of smoky fog which is bad news for people with asthma and breathing problems. The water vapour in the air condenses on to tiny particles given off by cars, factories and power stations. This makes the fog more dense and it is called smog. It forms more easily than fog and is slower to clear away.

Did you know that London used to have fog so thick that people could not see further than the ends of their arms? These terrible fogs were caused by smoke pollution and were called 'pea-soupers'.

Why is my snowball hard?

Fresh snow is made up of delicate crystals of ice with lots of air between them. When you press the snow together to make a snowball, you crush the ice crystals, pushing them closer together and making them melt. The water runs into all the gaps and freezes again into ice. So a snowball is made up of tiny bits of snow stuck together with ice – more of an iceball than a snowball. Ice is very hard, which is why snowballs are hard.

Did you know that an American farmer called 'Snowflake' Bentley spent 40 years taking magnified photos of thousands of snowflakes but never found two the same? Most snowflake patterns do have six sides, though.

Why do snowflakes have beautiful patterns?

Snowflakes are formed inside clouds when tiny drops of water freeze into ice crystals. Many crystals join together to make a snowflake. The shape and size of the flakes depends on the temperature, the amount of water in the cloud, and the height at which the flakes are formed. For instance, warmer temperatures cause star or plate shapes; colder temperatures produce rod- or needle-shaped flakes.

Why does my sledge sink into the snow?

Light, fluffy, fresh snow has a lot of air trapped in it because the pointed flakes do not fit together very well. Fresh snow is sometimes called powder snow. When you sit on your sledge, you push out the air and the sledge sinks down into the snow. Below the runners, ice may form, making it easier to slide along.

Why is snow white?

Light bounces back from the six sides of each snow crystal into your eyes. This is called reflection, and it makes the snow sparkle and look white. Snow is often slow to melt because it reflects away most of the sunlight falling on it.

Did you know that the snowiest place ever recorded is Paradise, in Mount Rainier National Park in the USA? Thirty-one metres of snow once fell there in one year!

Why can I slide on the ice?

Ice is very flat and smooth with few lumps and bumps in it. This means it causes very little friction when you walk on it. Friction is the force that holds things back when two surfaces rub against each other. When you walk on ice it is hard to stop yourself slipping over, even though making an ice slide is fun!

Did you know that the biggest hailstone so far recorded weighed as much as a bag of sugar? Luckily, most hailstones are about the size of a pea!

What are hailstones?

Hailstones are frozen raindrops that rise and fall inside storm clouds, becoming coated with several layers of ice. By cutting a hailstone in half and counting the layers, you can tell how many times it was tossed up and down inside a cloud. Hailstones swoop up and down in clouds at speeds of about 30 metres per second. Some hailstones are heavy enough to dent cars and break windows.

Why do some animals turn white in winter?

A white coat of fur or feathers is useful to animals that are out and about in winter because it makes them hard to see against a snowy background. This is called camouflage. It helps predators to creep up on the animals they eat without being seen, and it also lets the animals they hunt escape capture. The colour change is triggered when the weather gets colder and is sometimes quite sudden.

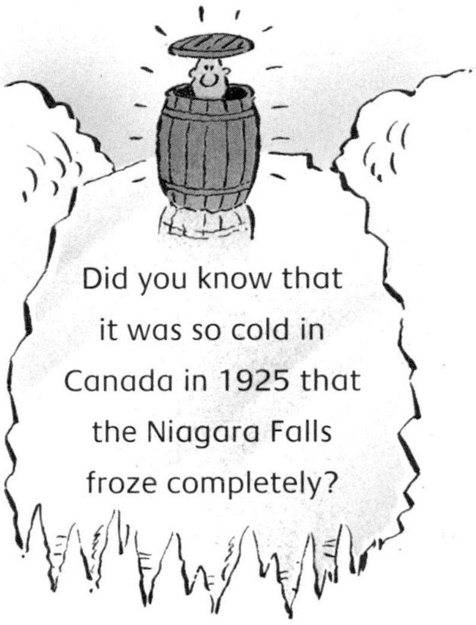

Did you know that it was so cold in Canada in 1925 that the Niagara Falls froze completely?

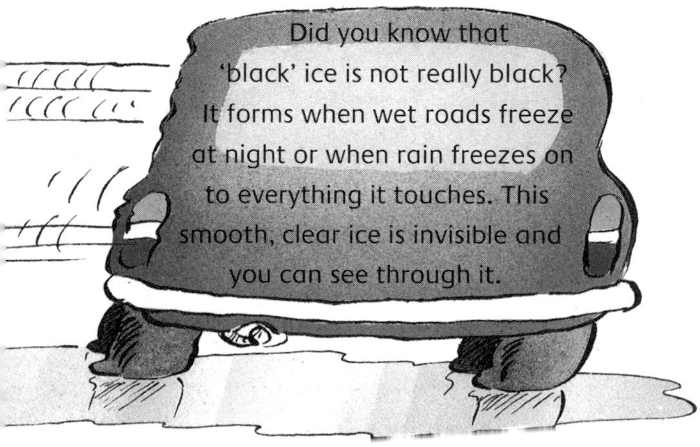

Did you know that 'black' ice is not really black? It forms when wet roads freeze at night or when rain freezes on to everything it touches. This smooth, clear ice is invisible and you can see through it.

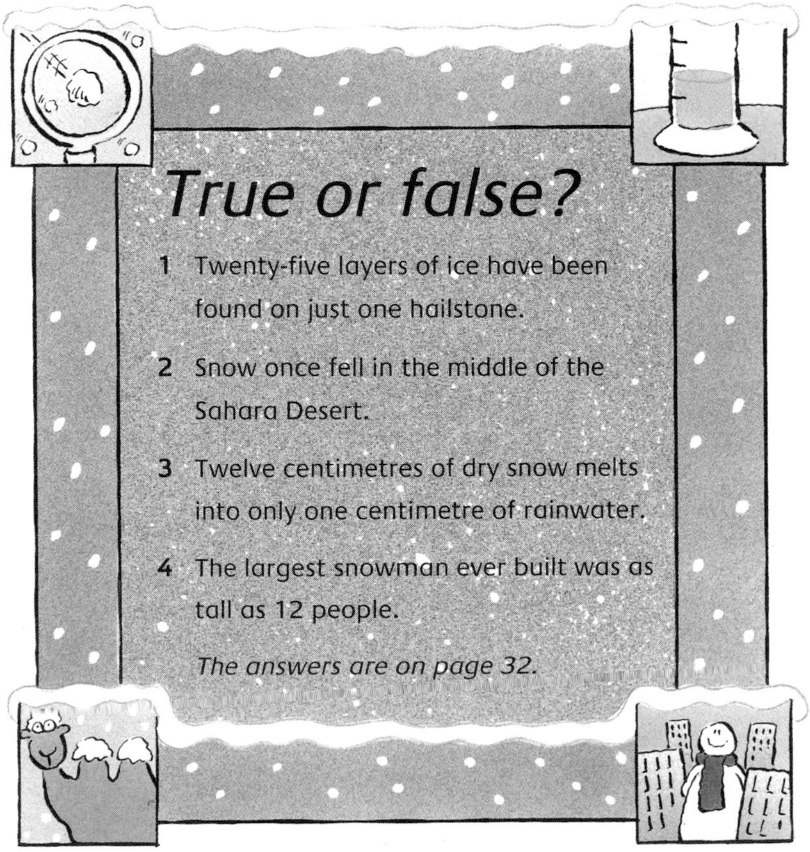

True or false?

1. Twenty-five layers of ice have been found on just one hailstone.
2. Snow once fell in the middle of the Sahara Desert.
3. Twelve centimetres of dry snow melts into only one centimetre of rainwater.
4. The largest snowman ever built was as tall as 12 people.

The answers are on page 32.

How can computers forecast the weather?

Information about the weather comes from thousands of weather stations and radar dishes on land, ships at sea, weather balloons in the sky and satellites out in space. All this data is fed into super-computers that can work out how the weather is likely to change. But the weather is very complex, and even with computers, it is hard to forecast accurately for more than a week or so ahead.

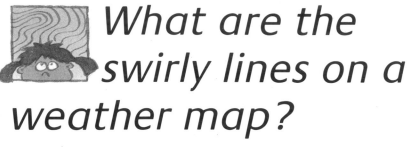

What are the swirly lines on a weather map?

The thinner swirly lines on a weather map are called isobars. When the isobars are close together, it means strong winds. When they are further apart, the winds are lighter. Isobars join up places that have the same air pressure. Although you can't feel or see it, the air around you presses down all the time on you and everything around you. When the air presses down hard, it makes high-pressure – the highs on a weather map. Highs mean good weather. When air pressure is low, it means bad weather.

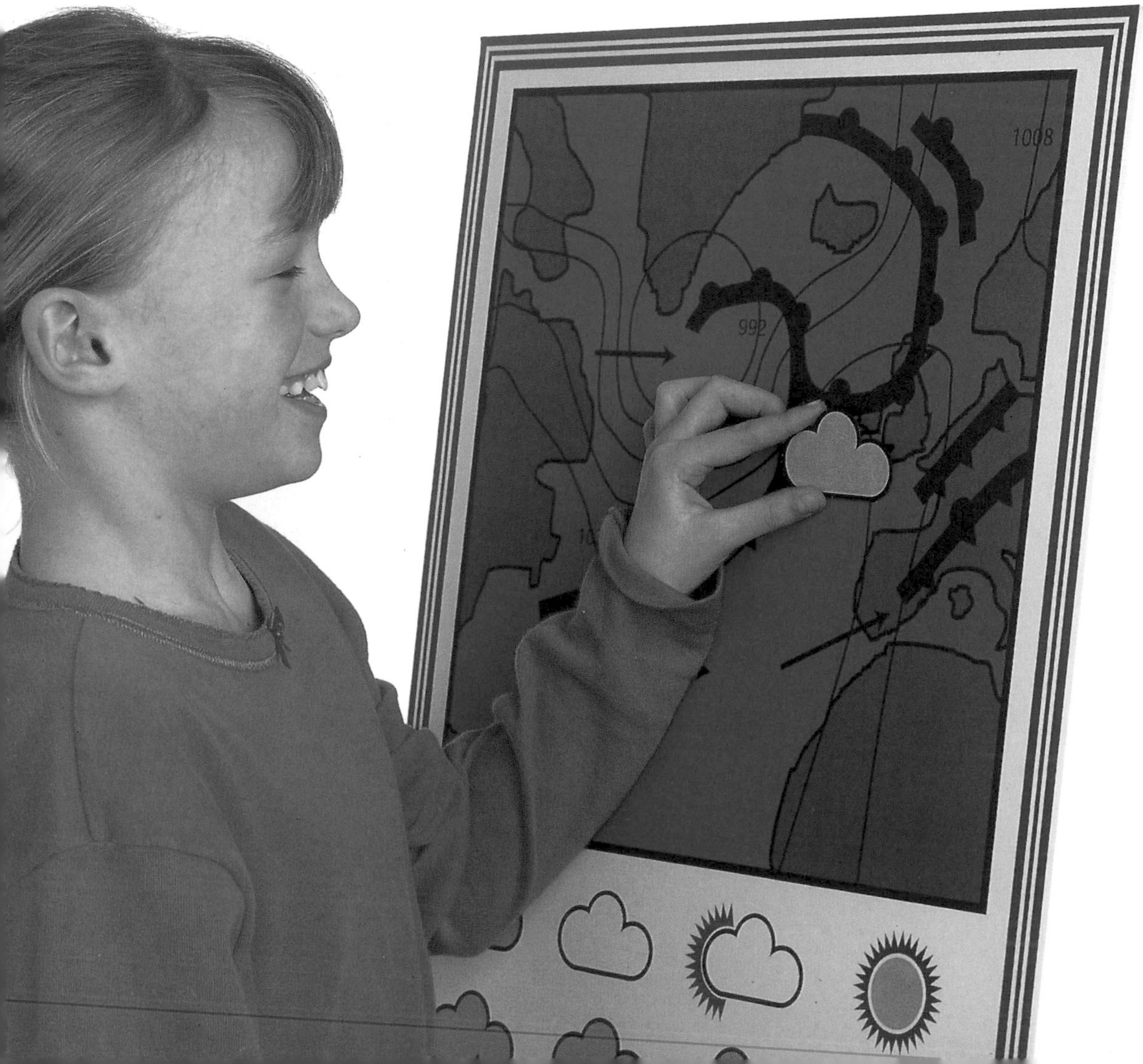

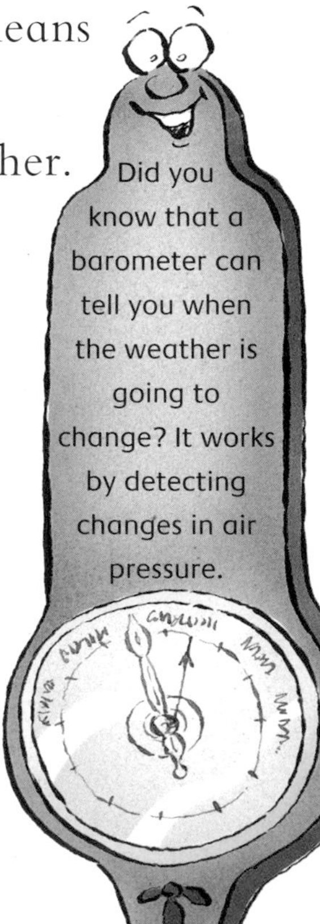

Did you know that a barometer can tell you when the weather is going to change? It works by detecting changes in air pressure.

How can pine-cones forecast the weather?

When the weather is dry, the scales on a pine-cone shrivel and unfold. This is because the pine-cones normally open their scales in dry weather to let the wind blow away their seeds. In wet weather, the scales take in moisture, swell and close up again. Which of the pine-cones above shows wet weather and which shows dry weather?

Did you know that groundhogs help people forecast the weather in North America? February 2nd is Groundhog Day. If the groundhog sees its shadow on this day, it is said that there will be six more weeks of winter.

How do animals know when the weather is going to change?

Animals are more sensitive to changes in air pressure or the amount of moisture in the air than people are. Dogs and farm animals are often restless before storms, and frogs croak when the air pressure drops. When it is going to rain, some people claim that cows lie down, or donkeys bray loudly.

How fast can the wind blow?

The fastest winds blow in violent storms called hurricanes and tornadoes. In a hurricane, winds blow in a spiral at up to 360 kph. Tornadoes are whirlwinds that can suck up people and vehicles like a vacuum cleaner. These winds can blow at over 400 kph.

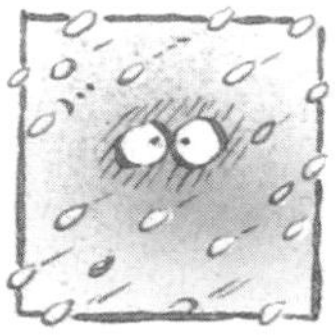

What happens in a blizzard?

A blizzard is a heavy winter snowstorm with strong winds, low temperatures and lots of fine, powdery snow. The broad, flat snowflakes are like little sails, so the wind catches them and makes them fly through the air fast. Winds in a severe blizzard reach over 72 kph and the blowing snow makes it impossible to see anything. Temperatures may be minus 12°C or lower. Snow can pile up in huge drifts and can completely cover cars and trains, trapping people inside.

Did you know that a tornado once lifted a railway carriage with passengers inside over 20 metres into the air?

wet winds blow off the sea

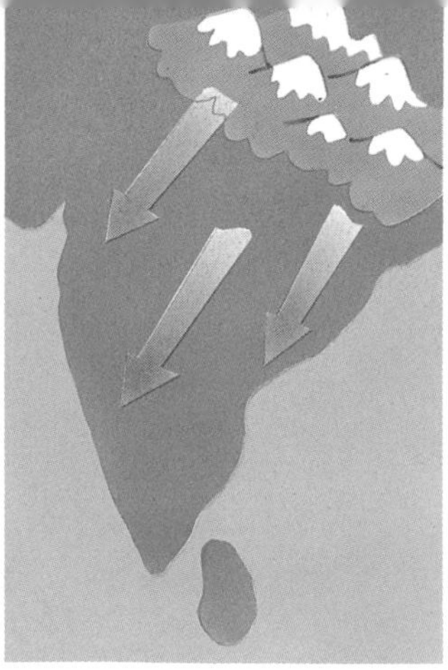

dry winds blow off the land

What is a monsoon?

The monsoon winds of India and other parts of Asia blow from opposite directions in different seasons. Heavy rains and floods happen when the winds blow off the sea and are full of moisture. As these winds rise over high ground, they cool down, forming the clouds that cause the heavy rainfall. When the monsoon winds blow the other way, off the dry land towards the sea, the weather is dry too.

What causes a flood?

Most floods happen when a lot of rain falls or a lot of snow melts and there is too much water to drain away. Rivers may burst over their banks, flooding the land nearby. Flooding also happens when the sea level rises, or when storms cause huge waves that swamp the coast. When rain is very heavy, all the water may rush over the land in a violent flash flood.

True or false?

1 Tornadoes can make buildings explode.

2 Flash floods are caused by flashes of lightning.

3 Hurricanes are named after famous people.

The answers are on page 32.

Why is thunder so loud?

During a thunderstorm, flashes of lightning heat up the air to incredible temperatures – five times as hot as the surface of the Sun. This heat makes the air suddenly spread out, or expand, at supersonic speed, which produces the deafening crash we call thunder. It's rather like the boom you hear when a supersonic aircraft like Concorde flies overhead.

Did you know that the Indonesian island of Java is the most thundery place in the world? It has thunder on about 300 days of the year.

How far away is the storm?

Lightning and thunder happen at the same time, but lightning travels much faster than the sound of thunder. This is why you often see lightning before you hear thunder. To find out how far away a storm is, in kilometres, count the seconds between the lightning and the thunder and divide by 2.5.

How does lightning jump out of clouds?

Lightning is a way of releasing the electrical energy that builds up inside thunderclouds. The energy at the bottom of the cloud is different from the energy at the top of the cloud, or the energy on the ground. When the lightning jumps down to the ground or to the top of a thundercloud, it evens out this difference in energy. Lightning jumping within clouds is called sheet lightning. Lightning jumping down to the ground is called fork lightning.

Lightning jumps down to the ground and then back up to the cloud again along the same path.

What is a flash of lightning?

Did you know that a light bulb would have to shine for 10,000 years to release the same amount of energy as one flash of lightning?

A flash of lightning is a spark of electricity zig-zagging to and fro between a thundercloud and the ground, or between two clouds. Electricity is made inside tall thunderclouds when water droplets and ice crystals are tossed up and down by winds and rub against each other. This sort of electricity is called static electricity. Rubbing a balloon against your hair makes electricity in the same way. The electric charge pulls your hair so it sticks to the balloon.

Did you know that the Earth's atmosphere stretches up about 1000 kilometres into space? It would take you almost two weeks to walk straight up into outer space!

Why does the Earth have an atmosphere?

The Earth has weather because it holds a blanket of gases called the atmosphere around itself. The Earth can do this because it gives off a strong pulling force called gravity, which pulls everything on Earth down to the ground. The gases in the Earth's atmosphere have mostly come from volcanoes or plants.

Is there weather on the Moon?

For weather to happen, there has to be air, water and heat. The Moon does not have a blanket of air around it as the Earth does. This is because the pulling force of the Moon's gravity is too weak to hold any air around it. The Moon also has no water. So although the Sun heats the Moon, there is no air and water to make the weather. Astronauts have to take their own air and water to the Moon, otherwise they would not be able to breathe or drink.

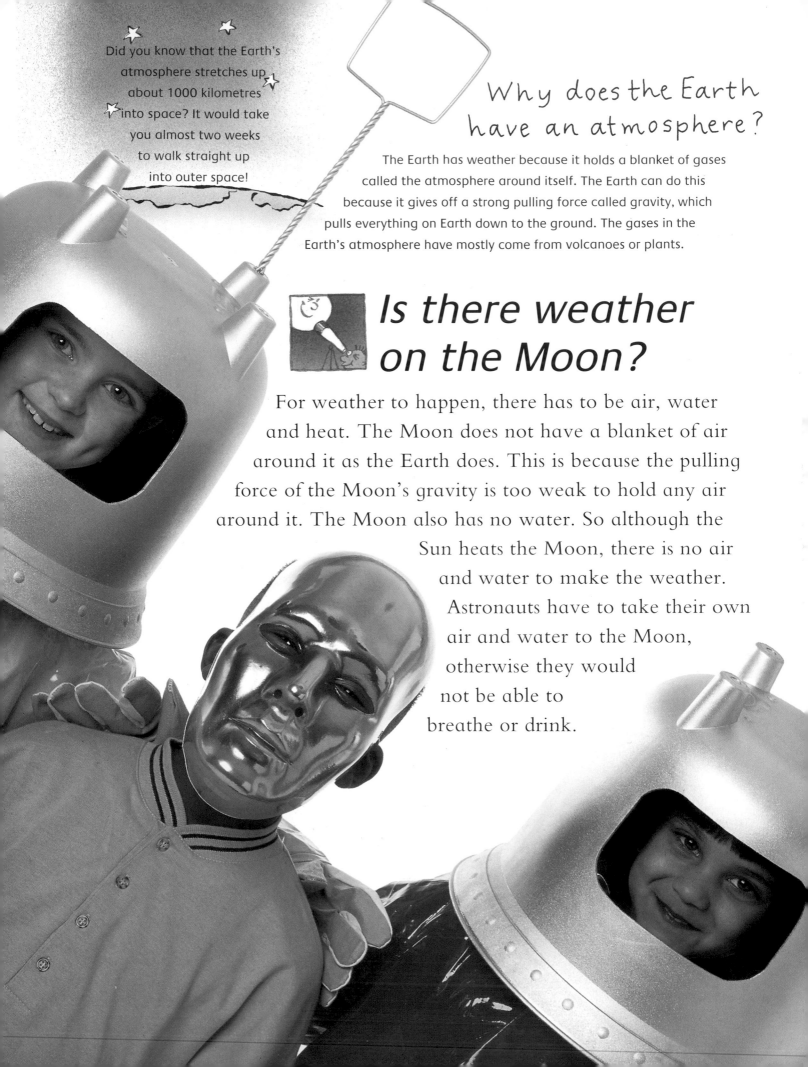

Why are some planets hot and some cold?

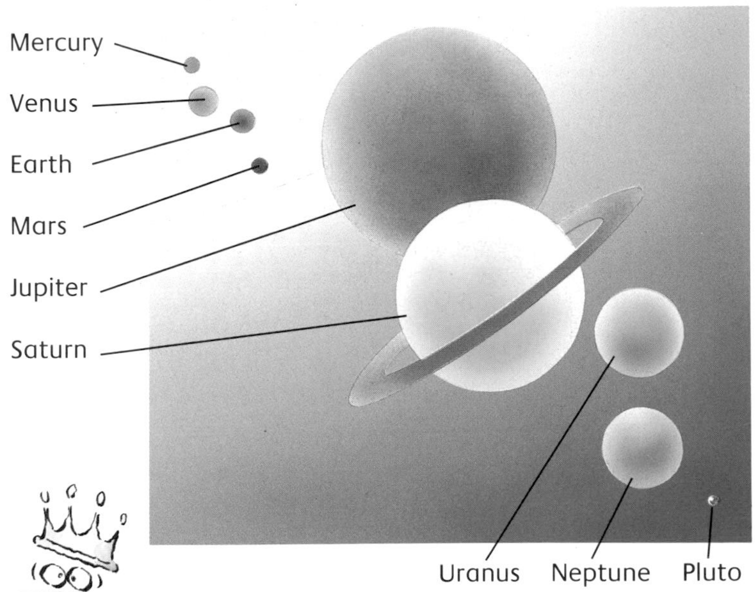
Mercury
Venus
Earth
Mars
Jupiter
Saturn
Uranus
Neptune
Pluto

The temperature on the planets in our solar system depends on how far they are from our Sun and on the mixture of gases in their atmospheres. Mercury is closest to the Sun, but it is not the hottest planet because it has very weak gravity and almost no atmosphere. Venus, next to Mercury, is the hottest planet. Temperatures on Venus reach up to 480°C because gases in its atmosphere act like a greenhouse and stop heat escaping. Further away from the Sun, the Earth is cooler than Venus, and Mars is cooler than the Earth.

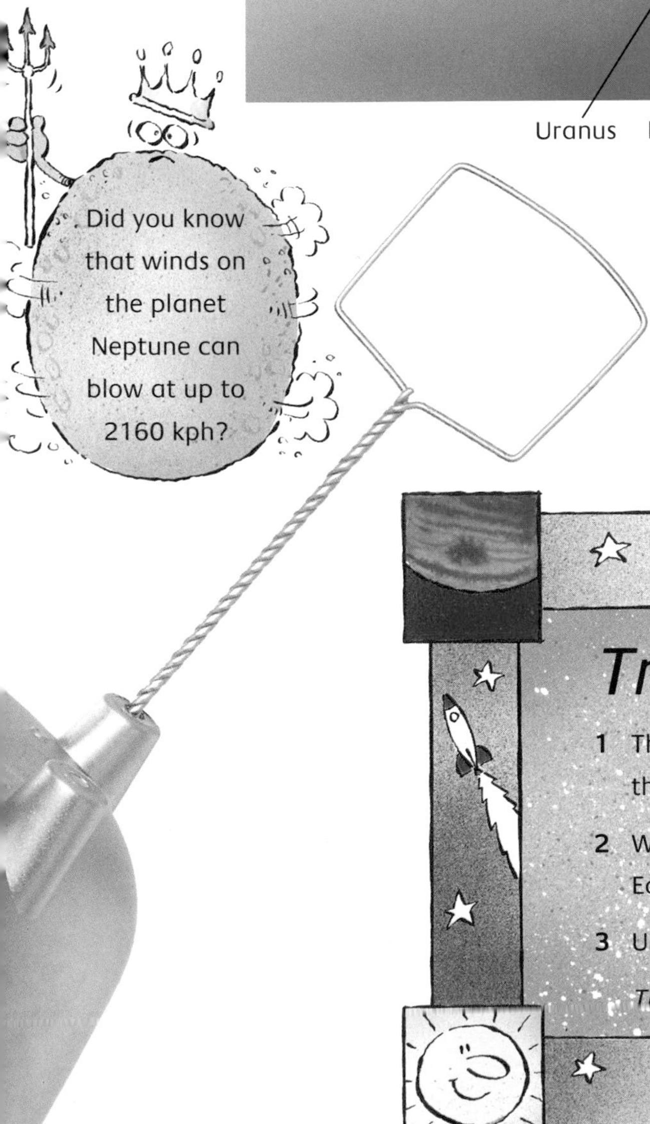
Did you know that winds on the planet Neptune can blow at up to 2160 kph?

True or false?

1 The red spot on Jupiter is a huge hurricane more than twice the size of the Earth.

2 Weather only happens in the bottom ten kilometres of the Earth's atmosphere.

3 Uranus receives about half as much sunlight as the Earth.

The answers are on page 32.

More about weather science

While you are watching or recording the weather, you are finding out about all kinds of science, from reflection, temperature and evaporation to air pressure, electricity and the Earth in space. Across these two pages you can find out about some of the most important science ideas in this book.

1 When light bounces off things, this is called **reflection**.

2 The 'bending' of light rays when they pass from one transparent material to another is called **refraction**.

When light bends in warm air, people may see far-away things in the wrong place. This is called a **mirage**.

3 A **shadow** is a dark area that forms behind an object when it blocks out the light.

4 Regular changes in the weather throughout the year are called **seasons**.

The imaginary line around the middle of the Earth is called the **equator**.

When liquid water is heated, it **evaporates** and changes into a gas called water vapour. When water vapour cools down, it **condenses** back into liquid water again. Clouds form because of water condensing.

5 A **cloud** is a mass of tiny droplets of water or ice crystals hanging in the air.

Fog is masses of tiny water droplets hanging in the air near the ground.

6 A **crystal** is a solid substance that has a regular shape outside because the particles inside are arranged in a regular pattern.

7 When two surfaces rub against each other, a force called **friction** slows them down or stops them moving.

The weight of air in the Earth's atmosphere pressing down on the Earth's surface is called **air pressure**.

The lines on a weather map joining places with the same air pressure are called **isobars.**

8 **Wind** is air moving from areas of high pressure to areas of low pressure. An **anemometer** measures wind speed.

A storm that has driving snow rather than rain is called a **blizzard**.

A violent tropical storm that forms over the west Atlantic Ocean is called a **hurricane**.

A **tornado** is a very violent, whirling storm that happens over land.

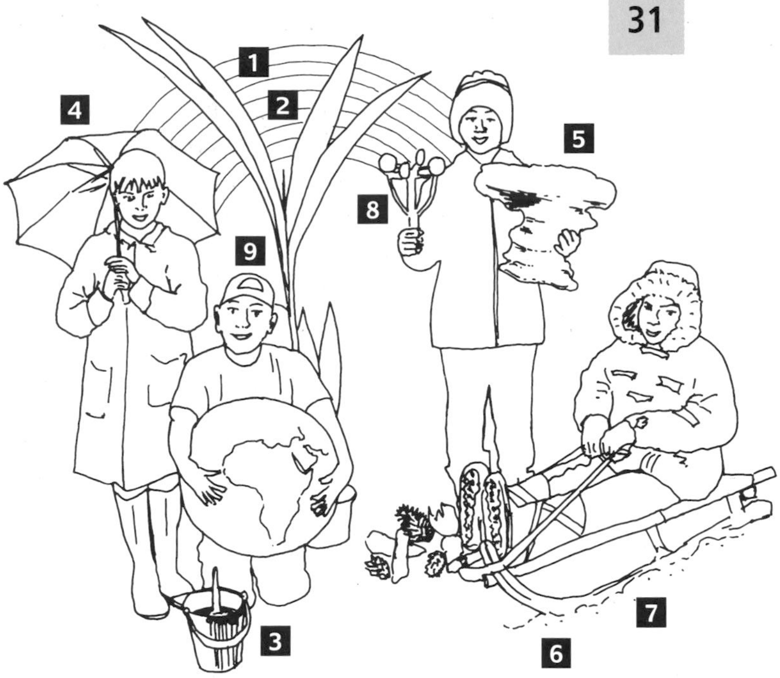

9 **Temperature** is how hot or how cold things are. This is measured using an instrument called a **thermometer.**

The **ozone layer** is made up of a form of oxygen called ozone. It surrounds the Earth and soaks up (absorbs) most of the Sun's harmful ultra-violet rays.

Invisible **ultra-violet rays** from the Sun make you sun-tanned, but too many of them are harmful to living things.

A **rainforest** is a thick forest that grows near the equator, where the climate is hot and wet all the year round.

Electricity is a form of energy. When some materials are rubbed together, they produce static electricity. A flash of **lightning** is static electricity.

Gravity is an invisible force pulling things down to the ground.

The thin 'skin' of gases around a planet is called its **atmosphere**.

The Sun and all the objects circling around it (such as the planets), are called the **solar system**.

A **planet** is a large ball of rock, metal or gas that moves around (orbits) a star such as the Sun.

Answers to quizzes

Page

9 **1** False. They are too big, and glue does not stick to air! **2** False. When dinosaurs were alive, the weather was much warmer than it is today; **3** True. They chirp at different speeds, depending on the temperature. If you count the number of chirps per minute and divide by four, then add 40, this gives you, very roughly, the temperature in degrees fahrenheit; **4** True.

14 **1** True, although no-one is quite sure why this happens; **2** False. Before 1971, no rain fell in this desert for over 400 years! **3** True. There is no water in the air in a clear sky, so rain cannot fall out of a clear, blue sky.

21 **1** True; **2** True. This happened in 1925; **3** True; **4** False. It was only as tall as three people, but was very tubby at 3.75 metres round the middle!

25 **1** True. The air pressure inside the funnel of a tornado is very low, and the air pressure inside a building is much higher. The difference in air pressure causes the explosion; **2** False. They are caused by sudden, very heavy rain which does not drain away; **3** False. They are each given names, though – alternately male and female.

29 **1** True. It is the biggest hurricane in the solar system; **2** True. This lowest layer of the atmosphere is called the troposphere; **3** False. It receives about 370 times less sunlight.

Index